D0010584

CARTOON·NATION

EST. presents 1776

# THE U.S. CONGRESS

by Eric Fein

illustrated by Brian Bascle

CONSULTANT:

Michael Bailey
Colonel William J. Walsh Associate Professor
of American Government
Georgetown University, Washington, D.C.

Capstone
press.

Mankato, Minnesota

Graphic Library is published by Capstone Press,
151 Good Counsel Drive, P.O. Box 669, Mankato, Minnesota 56002.
www.capstonepress.com

Copyright © 2008 by Capstone Press, a Capstone Publishers company. All rights reserved.
No part of this publication may be reproduced in whole or in part, or stored in a
retrieval system, or transmitted in any form or by any means, electronic, mechanical,
photocopying, recording, or otherwise, without written permission of the publisher.
For information regarding permission, write to Capstone Press, 151 Good Counsel Drive,
P.O. Box 669, Dept. R, Mankato, Minnesota 56002.
Printed in the United States of America

1 2 3 4 5 6 13 12 11 10 09 08

*Library of Congress Cataloging-in-Publication Data*
Fein, Eric.
  The U.S. Congress / by Eric Fein; illustrated by Brian Bascle.
  p. cm. — (Graphic Library. Cartoon nation)
  Summary: "In cartoon format, explains the history, role, and responsibilities of
Congress in United States government" — Provided by publisher.
  Includes bibliographical references and index.
  ISBN-13: 978-1-4296-1335-4 (hardcover)
  ISBN-10: 1-4296-1335-1 (hardcover)
  ISBN-13: 978-1-4296-1783-3 (softcover pbk.)
  ISBN-10: 1-4296-1783-7 (softcover pbk.)
  1.  United States. Congress — Juvenile literature. I. Bascle, Brian, ill. II. Title.
III. Series.
JK1025.F44 2008
328.73 — dc22                                                      2007031038

*Art Direction and Design*
Bob Lentz

*Cover Artist*
Kelly Brown

*Editor*
Christine Peterson

# TABLE OF CONTENTS

Welcome to Washington, D.C., home of the U.S. government. This capital city is where you will find senators, representatives, and other government leaders who like to talk a lot.

Elected lawmakers from each state meet at the Capitol. This building crackles with energy and ideas as lawmakers deal with issues facing the country.

## CONGRESS BY THE NUMBERS

The Senate and House of Representatives are not the same size. Each has a different number of lawmakers. The Senate has 100 members — two senators from each state. The House of Representatives has 435 members.

The U.S. Congress is made up of the Senate and the House of Representatives. Both groups help make laws for the country, but the Senate and House each have their own jobs to do. Like players in an orchestra, members of Congress need to work together.

But when lawmakers don't work in harmony, they can make quite a racket.

Lawmakers discuss everything from spending government money to video games to global warming. They track down information that will help them solve problems facing the nation.

The U.S. government is made up of three parts called branches. Each branch does its part to help run the country. The three branches also work together to make a strong national government.

The president leads the executive branch of government. However, the president doesn't work alone. Many advisers, including members of the cabinet, help the president make decisions.

Congress heads up the legislative branch. Congress passes taxes and makes laws that govern the country.

Somebody needs to make sure laws follow the **Constitution**. That job falls to the judicial branch and its Supreme Court. The Supreme Court reviews laws to make sure they are applied in a fair manner. The Court also makes sure presidential treaties and other acts follow the Constitution.

Constitution — the system of laws that state the rights of the people and the powers of the government

## CAPITAL CITY

In 1791, President George Washington chose the spot where the country's new capital city would be built. He chose an area of 100 square miles (259 square kilometers) along the Potomac River. The spot included land from Maryland and Virginia.

After the Revolutionary War (1775-1783), leaders of the new United States met in Philadelphia to form a strong national government. These leaders believed that no one person or group should control the country. They wanted the people to have a say in their government.

Ready, set, write!

During the hot summer of 1787, the delegates wrote the U.S. Constitution. This historic document explains how the government works.

Let's strike a deal before we all melt away.

Delegates argued about how many representatives each state should have. Delegates from large states wanted the number of representatives based on population. Those from small states wanted the same number of representatives from all states.

After weeks of hot and hearty debate, delegates finally agreed to a compromise. States would have an equal number of representatives in the Senate. In the House, the number of representatives would be based on a state's population.

## CONSTITUTION FACTS

The Constitution became law on June 21, 1788, after nine of the 13 states voted to approve it.

George Washington and James Madison were the only signers of the Constitution who later became U.S. presidents.

The original Constitution is displayed at the National Archives in Washington, D.C.

What does it take to be a representative or senator? Candidates for Congress must follow strict rules to get their names on ballots.

In the House, representatives must be at least 25 years old and be U.S. citizens for the past seven years. They must live in the state they represent.

Representatives are elected to two-year **terms**. House members can be elected again.

In the Senate, senators must be 30 years old and U.S. citizens for the past nine years. They also must live in the state they represent. Senators serve six-year terms. When their term is up, senators can run for reelection.

Before joining Congress, many senators and representatives worked as lawyers. But that doesn't mean you need a law degree and an itchy suit to join Congress. Restaurant owners, doctors, and retired military people have all served in Congress. So has a former First Lady. A professional basketball player and an astronaut also served as senators.

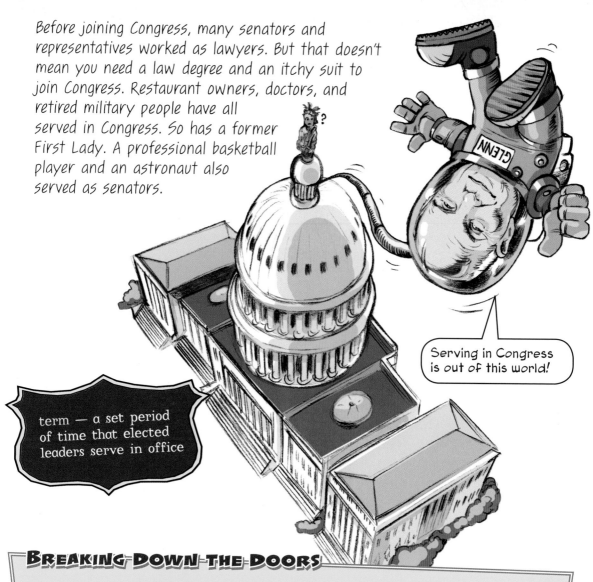

Serving in Congress is out of this world!

term — a set period of time that elected leaders serve in office

## BREAKING DOWN THE DOORS

For many years, only white males could be elected to Congress. Today, almost anyone can run for office. Here are some people who broke down the doors to Congress:

In 1822, Joseph Marion Hernández became the first Hispanic elected to Congress. Hernández was elected as a delegate from Florida, which was a U.S. territory at that time.

In 1870, Hiram Revels of Mississippi became the first African American elected to Congress.

In 1916, Jeannette Rankin of Montana became the first woman elected to Congress.

In 2007, Nancy Pelosi of California became the first woman to serve as the Speaker of the House.

Most candidates are members of a **political party**. Many political parties work in the United States, but the Democratic and Republican parties are the largest. Independent and third party candidates don't belong to a major political party.

During the election season, candidates spend big bucks to get their ideas out to voters. They crisscross their home states by plane, train, car, or even bike to meet with citizens.

political party — a group of people who share the same beliefs about how the government should operate

During election season, it seems like candidates are on TV all the time. Every channel. Every hour. Every minute. Some candidates start campaigning more than a year before the election is held! You hear them on the radio and read about them in newspapers.

After all the speeches and TV commercials, it's the voters' turn to decide. Every two years in November, citizens cast their ballots and elect lawmakers to represent them in Congress.

Once they're elected, members of Congress find themselves buried in work. It's like having homework seven days a week! So what's the main job of Congress? To make laws for our country.

Woo-Hoo! Let the lawmaking begin!

THE BRAND NEW SENATOR

STUFF

MORE STUFF

Congress passes laws that give money to schools and protect the environment. Congress also makes rules for becoming a new citizen.

Now this is money well spent.

SCHOOL

## MONEY, MONEY

Do you have some money tucked away in a piggy bank or savings account? Well, it was Congress that made sure the money got printed.

Congress also has the power to declare war. Lawmakers take this power very seriously. Congress has only officially declared war five times in U.S. history.

## WARS DECLARED BY CONGRESS

War of 1812 (1812–1815)

Mexican War (1846–1848)

Spanish–American War (1898)

World War I (1914–1918)

World War II (1939–1945)

Congress sometimes supports military action in other countries without declaring war.

The House and Senate have separate duties as well. The House introduces laws about taxes. Senators review the president's choices for the cabinet and Supreme Court. Senators also approve the president's treaties with other countries.

Better luck next time, Mr. President.

NOMINEE

Rats!

## LEADERS OF CONGRESS

The Speaker of the House leads the House of Representatives. The Speaker is a member of the political party that has the most members in the House. In the Senate, the vice president serves as president of the Senate. However, the vice president only votes if there is a tie. In the Senate, the majority leader has powers similar to the Speaker of the House.

Each year, thousands of **bills** are introduced in Congress, but only a few become laws. Bills get their start as an idea from a citizen, group, or lawmaker. Representatives and senators then introduce these ideas as bills in Congress.

Bill, I'd like you to meet the members of Congress.

Whoa. This looks like a tough crowd.

In the House and Senate, bills follow similar paths on the journey to becoming laws. After a bill is introduced, it gets sent to a committee. Committee members review the bill and make changes. Then the House and Senate vote on the bill.

Hold still. We need to make a few changes, so you'll be a better fit.

Hey, watch it with that pin, fella!

bill — a written plan for a new law that is discussed and voted on for approval

But if the committee decides the bill isn't strong enough, it gets tossed out like yesterday's trash.

Aw, this is no way to treat a friend.

In most cases, the House and Senate each pass their own version of a bill. These two bills then go before a committee of representatives and senators. This group works out the differences between the two bills.

Once the committee agrees on changes, the final bill goes before the House and Senate for another vote. If Congress passes the bill, it gets sent to the president. If the president signs the bill, it becomes a new law.

## VETO POWER

If presidents don't agree with new bills, they have the power to veto, or reject them. When the president vetoes a bill, it goes back to Congress. Congress can override a veto if two-thirds of its members vote in favor of the bill.

If each one of Congress' 535 members worked on every bill, nothing would ever get done. The government would come to a grinding halt.

To keep our government moving, Congress divides its work between committees. Senate and House committees act like sports teams. But instead of winning a game, they work to get laws passed.

Congress has several committees that tackle different issues. Standing committees are permanent groups that handle issues such as money or the military. Joint committees include House and Senate members. Committees also have their own smaller groups called subcommittees.

The House has 20 standing committees. One of the largest is the Appropriations Committee. This group reviews plans for spending government money.

Let's spend these dollars on the environment . . .

. . . and these on new roads.

The Senate has 16 standing committees, including the Armed Services Committee. This group provides money and equipment for the military.

# A CAPITOL TOUR

Lawmakers work 10 to 12 hours a day and sometimes longer. Lawmakers begin their day with office work and committee meetings. Before breakfast, their cell phones are bursting with text messages and voice mails.

Sometimes meetings are scheduled at the same time. Members of Congress can't be in two places at once. Aides sometimes attend meetings and report back to representatives or senators. Lawmakers then follow up with phone calls and e-mails to make sure they're on top of the issues.

Strap on your running shoes. We've got a marathon day ahead.

COMMITTEE ROOMS

A    B    C

Representatives and senators spend hours answering phone calls, letters, and e-mails. They meet with people from their home state. Lawmakers help shape bills to benefit their home states and the nation.

Congress members have several staff members to help with their heavy workloads. Each lawmaker has about 40 to 50 assistants both in their Washington, D.C., and state offices.

## BATTER UP!

Of course, it's not all work and no play in Congress. Lawmakers find ways to help their community as well. Since 1909, lawmakers have competed in an annual baseball game. The game pits Republicans against Democrats. The game doesn't settle any political differences, but it does raise money for charities in the Washington, D.C., area.

As the country grew and changed, Congress faced new challenges. Over the years, Congress acted to advance the rights of citizens and protect the country.

In 1789, Congress proposed 12 **amendments** to the Constitution. By 1791, states had adopted 10 of these amendments, which became the Bill of Rights. These amendments established the basic rights of U.S. citizens, including freedom of religion and speech.

In 1865, the United States was nearing the end of the Civil War. Congress took action to settle the issue of slavery that had divided the nation. That year, Congress proposed the 13th Amendment outlawing slavery in all states. The amendment became law on December 6, 1865.

On February 19, 1869, Congress proposed the 15th Amendment to give African American men the right to vote. The amendment became law on February 3, 1870.

amendment — a change made to a law or a legal document

Voting rights remained a national issue. In the early 1900s, women protested and petitioned Congress for the right to vote. In 1919, Congress proposed the 19th Amendment to extend voting rights to women. States approved the amendment on August 18, 1920.

In December 1941, Japan attacked the U.S. military base of Pearl Harbor in Hawaii. Following the attack, Congress declared war on Japan and the United States officially entered World War II (1939-1945).

In 1964, Congress passed the Civil Rights Act to protect African Americans and other minorities from discrimination in public places and on the job.

Congress has accomplished a lot since 1789. But there's always more work to be done. Each day, members of Congress face new issues and challenges.

Congress started out small, just like the country. But Congress changed to meet the needs of a growing nation. When the first U.S. Congress met in 1789, it had just 87 members from 13 states.

Today, Congress has 535 members representing all 50 states. Each member makes sure people in their home state or district get their concerns heard in Washington, D.C. Lawmakers introduce laws or suggest changes to help people in their home state.

Lawmakers know that to keep their job in Congress, they must serve the needs of the people who elected them. That way, Congress remains the citizen's voice in government.

Just look at how hard Congress is working.

Well, they should be. I've got lots of ideas for them.

# Time Line

June 21, 1788 — The U.S. Constitution becomes law after two-thirds of the states vote in favor of the new government.

September 25, 1789 — Congress proposes 12 amendments to the U.S. Constitution. By 1791, states approve 10 of the amendments, creating the Bill of Rights.

## June 21, 1788

## September 25, 1789

January 31, 1865 — Congress proposes the 13th Amendment to the Constitution, outlawing slavery in the United States. The amendment becomes law on December 6 after winning approval from 27 states.

December 2, 1863 — Construction of the Statue of Freedom on the Capitol's dome is completed. The bronze statue of a woman stands 19 feet 6 inches (5.94 meters) high and weighs about 15,000 pounds (6,800 kilograms).

## December 2, 1863

## January 31, 1865

June 4, 1919 — Congress proposes the 19th Amendment to extend voting rights to women. The amendment is approved on August 18, 1920.

March 4, 1929 — The inauguration of Vice President Charles Curtis becomes the first radio broadcast from the Senate's chamber.

## June 4, 1919

## March 4, 1929

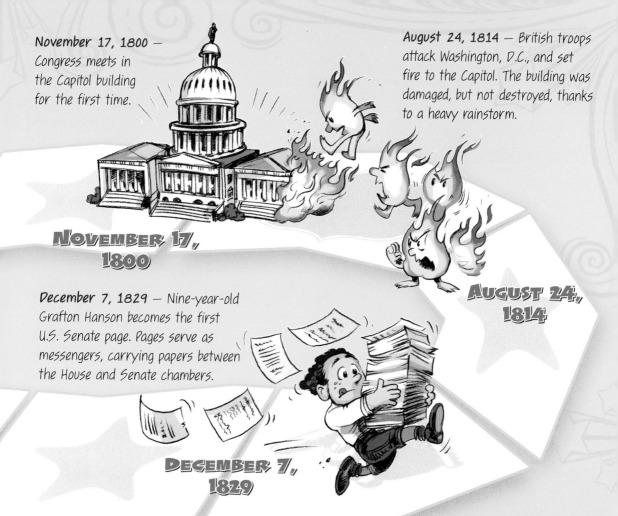

November 17, 1800 — Congress meets in the Capitol building for the first time.

**NOVEMBER 17, 1800**

August 24, 1814 — British troops attack Washington, D.C., and set fire to the Capitol. The building was damaged, but not destroyed, thanks to a heavy rainstorm.

**AUGUST 24, 1814**

December 7, 1829 — Nine-year-old Grafton Hanson becomes the first U.S. Senate page. Pages serve as messengers, carrying papers between the House and Senate chambers.

**DECEMBER 7, 1829**

July 2, 1964 — Congress passes the Civil Rights Act of 1964. The law protects African Americans and other minorities from discrimination in everyday life.

January 4, 2007 — Representative Nancy Pelosi of California becomes the first woman to serve as Speaker of the House.

Civil Rights Act 1964

**JULY 2, 1964**

**JANUARY 4, 2007**

# GLOSSARY

amendment (uh-MEND-muhnt) — a change made to a law or a legal document

bill (BIL) — a written plan for a new law that is discussed and voted on for approval or disapproval

candidate (KAN-duh-dayt) — a person who runs for elected office

Constitution (kon-stuh-TOO-shuhn) — the system of laws that state the rights of the people and the powers of the government

delegate (DEL-uh-guht) — a person chosen to speak and act for others

election (e-LEK-shuhn) — the process of choosing someone or deciding something by voting

political party (puh-LIT-uh-kuhl PAR-tee) — a group of people who share the same beliefs about how the government should operate

representative (rep-ri-ZEN-tuh-tiv) — a person elected to serve the government; U.S. representatives serve in the House.

senator (SEN-ah-tur) — a person elected to represent the people in the government; U.S. senators serve in the Senate.

term (TURM) — a set period of time that elected leaders serve in office

# READ MORE

Giddens-White, Bryon. *Congress and the Legislative Branch*. Our Government. Chicago: Heinemann, 2006.

Hamilton, John. *How a Bill Becomes a Law*. Government in Action!. Edina, Minn.: Abdo, 2005.

Horn, Geoffrey M. *The Congress*. World Almanac Library of American Government. Milwaukee: World Almanac Library, 2003.

O'Donnell, Liam. *Democracy*. Cartoon Nation. Mankato, Minn.: Capstone Press, 2008.

# INTERNET SITES

FactHound offers a safe, fun way to find Internet sites related to this book. All of the sites on FactHound have been researched by our staff.

Here's how:
1. Visit *www.facthound.com*
2. Choose your grade level.
3. Type in this book ID 1429613351 for age-appropriate sites. You may also browse subjects by clicking on letters, or by clicking on pictures and words.
4. Click on the Fetch It button.

FactHound will fetch the best sites for you!

# INDEX